The Porch Puppies

by Elizabeth M. Stevens

Published by Waldorf Publishing
2140 Hall Johnson Road
#102-345
Grapevine, Texas 76051
www.WaldorfPublishing.com

The Porch Puppies

ISBN: 978-1-64921-480-5

Library of Congress Control Number: 2020940330

Copyright © 2020

All rights reserved. No part of this book may be reproduced or transmitted in any form or by any means whatsoever without express written permission from the author, except in the case of brief quotations embodied in critical articles and reviews. Please refer all pertinent questions to the publisher. All rights reserved. No part of this book may be reproduced or transmitted in any form or by any means, electronic or mechanical, including photocopying, recording, or by an information storage and retrieval system except by a reviewer who may quote brief passages in a review to be printed in a magazine or newspaper without permission in writing from the publisher.

Illustrations by Ashley Kenny
Design by Baris Celik

The Porch Puppies is dedicated in loving memory of Lee and Meta Stevens. We don't get to pick our parents, nor the way we're born into this world.

I just got lucky.

Thank you, Mom and Dad.

Thank you to the family and friends who, through their many acts of kindness, inspired this story.

A special thank you to my sister, Kathy Verdi, and her second grade class at Faith Lutheran School for reading The Porch Puppies and sharing their thoughts about the book with me.

Table of Contents

Chapter 1
Special Delivery
The Discovery

Chapter 2
The Meeting
The Drive Home
The Capture

QUIZ
Then & Today

Chapter 3
Home Sweet Home
Vet Time
The Siblings are Reunited

Chapter 4
Our New Purpose
Sweetie and Yippy
And We Lived Happily Ever After

Puppy Love Song
Author Bio

Chapter 1

Special Delivery

It was a beautiful Friday morning in October. The sky was clear, the birds were singing, squirrels were chasing each other, and the humans worked happily as they dreamed of their weekend plans. But, in my world, the sun wasn't shining so brightly. Early that morning my brother, sisters and I had been scooped up, taken from our mother, and placed in the back of an old, green, beat-up truck. We didn't know where we were going or what was waiting for us when the truck stopped. We were frightened and lonely for our mother.

When we arrived at our destination, the driver shouted to his friend, "Harry, get those dogs out of the back."

"Where we gonna put them things?" Harry asked.

"Heck, I don't care, just as long as I get rid of them nuisances," Willy said.

"Well, I think I'll leave them on the porch," Harry laughed. "Sort of like getting a present from the Stork."

Harry placed the box that held my siblings and me onto the porch. I was happy to be out of the sun and thankful for the cool breeze. I missed my mother and I was hungry. I snuggled with my brother and sisters and we fell asleep.

"Arooo," cried the coyote.

"Uh....Dddid aanybody hear that?" I stammered.

"Yeah, sounds kind of close to me," Berry replied.

"We're not scared of you!" screeched Yippy. "Just try to get us you big, furry bag of bones!

"Quiet Yippy!" I said. "He sounds a lot bigger than we are!"

"Come on guys. Follow me," said our sister, Sweetie. "We'll sleep under the porch tonight. We'll be safe there."

Sweetie always took care of us. She was the oldest. I guess that's why she was so wise.

The Discovery

"Honey, come here!" Dr. Avery exclaimed. His wife, hearing the alarm in his voice, came quickly.

"Oh my......," she said, "Who could do such a thing? How could a person abandon these sweet, little puppies....with not even any water left for them to drink! I wonder how long they've been here? I'm so glad we came up this weekend to take care of chores! What might have happened to them had we not found them?....."

She seems nice! Could it be we've found a place to call home? I was hopeful!

"Honey, we can't keep them and if we feed them, they'll never leave," Dr. Avery said.

"Well, we can't let them starve," she replied. "They're puppies and they don't know how to provide for themselves. I'll leave them food and water in the back and before we leave, I'll ask our neighbor to care for them until we can find a place that can take them."

Dr. and Mrs. Avery called all the local animal shelters that weekend but none of them had room for us, so Dr. and Mrs. Avery decided to call their neighbor, Josh, to ask if he could help.

"Hello, Josh, this is Mrs. Avery."

"Hi there, Mrs. Avery. How are you?" Josh asked.

"We're fine. Hey, I have a huge favor to ask of you," she said. "Someone left four puppies on our porch. We found them when we arrived here on Friday. We called the shelters, but there's no room for them so we've been feeding and caring for them this weekend. Is there any chance you could continue to give them food and water until we can find them a home?"

"Sure. I'd be happy to. That sure was cruel to leave those puppies like that. I just don't understand how people can be so unkind," Josh replied.

"Yes, I agree. If you can't care for an animal you should always find it a good home," said Mrs. Avery.

After the Averys left to go back home, the neighbor did what he promised to do and brought us food and water every day.

Chapter 2

The Meeting

Aimee was a manager at work and was always buried in paper. One day, when Aimee was walking back to her office she overheard the doctor's conversation with his nurse. She was very upset to hear someone had abandoned us and wanted to know more.

"Yeah, sometime last week four puppies were dropped on our porch at the lake house," Dr. Avery said. "It's a good thing we were there last weekend. The puppies are fine, but they're pretty thin."

"Who's taking care of them now?" Aimee asked.

"Our neighbors, but al don't know what they're going to do with them. We called the animal shelters, but they're not taking any more strays."

"I can take them!" Aimee shouted with glee!

Aimee rushed to finish her work and took off. She stopped at a store and bought dog food, bottled water, and some bowls to hold the food and water she was bringing to us.

"Oh," she thought. "I hope I remember how to get there!" Aimee was never very good at remembering directions and was grateful she had a full tank of gas, a reliable car, and a charged cellphone lying beside her!

"This looks right... Oh yes, I remember that...". Two hours later she exclaimed, "I did it!" During the ride, Aimee had been thinking about how she was going to care for the puppies when she brought them home. She was excited to get a look at us and elated she had found the lake house without getting lost!

"Well, hi there! Are you hungry?" she asked us. "Look what I brought for you guys.... here you go....do you want some water?...."

I liked her voice! It was kind. She fed us, gave us water, and talked to us. But why was she being so nice? I moved closer to her little by little. She wanted to pet me, and I wanted her to pet me too, but I was afraid, so when I would get too close to her, I would run off.

Aimee stayed for a couple of hours. She seemed very nice, but abandonment by our owners had made us distrustful of humans despite her kindness to us. "Well guys, this isn't going to be as easy as I first thought," she said. "I'm going to need some help catching you boys and girls!"

Aimee turned to go to her car. The sun was setting, and she needed to leave. I kept a safe distance from her, followed her a little way, and then watched her drive away.

The Drive Home

"Dr. Avery, this is Aimee. I went to your lake house to get the pups, but they wouldn't come to me. They're really afraid of humans."

"Call our neighbors. They'll be happy to help you catch the dogs," Dr. Avery said.

Dr. Avery was right. Dr. and Mrs. Avery had very good neighbors. Before we lived with Aimee, they fed us, gave us clean water every day, and built us a cage with hay to keep us warm because the evenings were starting to get very cold.

Aimee called Josh and told him she was unable to catch us.

"Yeah, they won't get close to us either. They're eating the food we put down, but only after we leave. But don't worry, I can catch them for you. We've built a cage with hay to keep them warm and they all snuggle in there together and fall asleep at night. We can sneak up behind them while they're sleeping and close the gate. I know you have a trip coming up, so when you get back into town let me know when you're ready for them, and I'll put them in the back of my truck and drive them into town to you."

The Capture

When Aimee returned from her vacation, she called Josh to arrange to get us.

"Josh, it's Aimee. I'm back in town. Can you bring the pups tomorrow?"

"Hey, Aimee, sure thing. I'll call you when I get there and meet you in your garage at work."

Josh did exactly as he had promised. That night while my siblings and I were sleeping, he tip-toed up to the cage and closed the front door. "It's ok guys, go back to sleep," Josh said. "Tomorrow you're going to have a home....."

The next morning Josh drove us to where Aimee worked.

"Hi Josh! Thank you for bringing them here!" Aimee said.

"Well, I wasn't able to catch the big one. She seems to be a little more aware and suspicious than the others. Every time we got close to the cage she would take off. We'll get her, but it's going to take more time."

"Oh, look at those sweet pups...." Aimee said. "They're so frightened."

"Yeah, it's a good thing I wore these gloves," Josh said. Then grimacing a bit, "The little black one bit me!"

"I'll remember to let them smell my hand before I pick them up," Aimee said.

One by one, Aimee and Josh picked us up and put us in the back of Aimee's car. We were cold and shivering, but Aimee had placed blankets in the cage she had put in the back of her car to keep us warm. When we drove away, we didn't know where we were going, but something told me it was going to be a good place.

Chapter 3

Home Sweet Home

"What's that noise?... Why is it so dark in here?"... And then it was quiet. "Where did Aimee go?"....

"Ok guys, welcome to your new home!" Aimee said joyfully. "Did you wonder where I went? Well, I just had to put my dog, Callie, outside. You know, she isn't use to sharing her mama with anyone..... I'm not sure if she's going to be very happy to see you all! No worries though! She'll grow to love you!"

Aimee brought us into her home one by one and placed us inside the crate she had prepared in the kitchen. Oh, I loved my new home! I could smell all the other animals Aimee had taken care of, and I could feel warmth and happiness! After we were settled in our new home, Aimee brought in Callie. Callie came over to our cage and smelled all around us. "Hey, where did you all come from?" she barked. I told Callie we didn't have a home. "Well, you have one now," Callie said. "Just remember, I'm the boss!"

My siblings and I spent many happy days and nights in our new home. We always had food, water and treats. Aimee had many friends who came over to bathe us, play with us and take us for walks. Up until now, humans weren't creatures we particularly cared for, but I was learning there are as many different kinds of humans as there are dogs! And some of them are very, very nice! My tail wagged constantly! Sometimes, I could barely walk it was going so fast! I think that's why Aimee named me Happy. I've never heard a dog called that name before, but it sure was a good name for me. Yes, I was happy. I was very happy, and I never wanted to leave!

Vet Time

"Boys and girls, let's go!" Aimee placed us back into the crate she had in the back of her car.

"Hey Berry, where do you think we're going?" I asked.

"Gee, who knows," Berry answered. "But, I know Aimee loves us, so it must be somewhere good."

"I'd rather just stay home," Yippy said. "We're happy there...and it's cold out here!"

"Yeah....let's snuggle and keep each other warm," I said.

"Ok boys and girls, you're going to the vet today. Now, there's no need to be afraid. The vet is a very nice man, and he's going to make sure you stay healthy. Promise me you'll be good! I want him to think you're as wonderful as I do!"

"Oh dear....what's a vet?" Berry asked.

"Not sure, but I'm pretty sure we're not going to like it — or him" Yippy chimed in.

"I agree. I'm getting nervous," I said, "And my stomach isn't feeling very good."

"Oh Happy, what's that smell?" Yippy asked.

"Sorry," I replied. "My stomach hurts...."

"I think I'll move over here," Berry said. Berry moved as far away from me as he could get and buried his nose in the blanket.

Aimee drove us to the vet, talking to us the entire time. She was trying to help us stay calm, but we were too worried about what was waiting for us to be distracted by her chatter. When we arrived, the lady in the front greeted us warmly. She seemed to already know why we were there.

"Well, hello there!" she exclaimed. "You brought the porch puppies!"

"Yes, at least most of them," Aimee said. "The biggest one hasn't been caught yet."

"That's fine. You can bring her in when you can," the lady replied.

One by one she brought us to the back of the office where the vet examined us. He was very thorough and really very nice.... "Ouch! What was that for!"

"Sorry, young fellow," he said. "I have to give you a couple of vaccines so you'll stay healthy."

After a little while, he was done with me, and I was able to join my siblings out front.

"How was it?" Berry and Yippy asked.

"I didn't like the vacuum," I said.

"He vacuums you?" Yippy looked puzzled.

"No...well, it was something like that. It pinched!"

When we were all done, Aimee paid the bill with a credit card. I heard her tell the lady the doctor she worked for offered to pay the vet bills. Aimee told the lady sometimes it takes a village and that everybody was doing what they could to help us. The doctor had said he didn't have any time to care for us but offered to help by giving money.

"That's very generous of him," the lady said.

"Yes, yes, it is," Aimee replied.

I can't say I enjoyed going to the vet, but I admit he was quite kind. We all wanted to please Aimee and did our best to make a good impression, but I don't think we did a very good job. I confess I was very nervous and made a smelly mess....and Yippy was so scared she tried to bite him! And then, when we were leaving, I heard the vet tell Aimee she might want to give us some kind of medicine before she brought us there again so we would be calmer... Oh my..... there are going to be more of these trips????

When we arrived home, we ran outside to play in the yard. We were so excited to be home! We chased each other and we chased squirrels. When Aimee was done making our dinner, she brought us inside to eat. We ate our dinner and after our adventure at the vet, it tasted better than ever! I love my new home! Every morning I am so excited to get up because I know there's another new adventure waiting for me! But, I think my favorite time of the day is the evening when we sit on the couch, watch TV and cuddle.

The Siblings are Reunited

"Look who I have here!" Aimee joyfully exclaimed.

Josh had caught my sister, Sweetie, and brought her to Aimee's office a couple of weeks later. But when Aimee brought Sweetie home to join the family, I wasn't very excited to see her. I was happy she was going to be well cared for and loved a lot, but I admit I was a little jealous, too. She was sticking close to Aimee, and I didn't like it. Aimee had thought I'd be excited to see Sweetie because we played together all the time when we were at the lake. But, I had gotten accustomed to my new life. It was a good one, and it took me a little while to want to share it with my sister.

"Hey!" Sweetie called to me. "Why are you ignoring me?"

The words, "I'm...not...," stumbled out of my mouth.

"Yes, you are!" she exclaimed. "Seems to me you're seeing things all wrong here! You shouldn't be jealous of me! I can be your helper! I bet, if we put our heads together, we could trick Aimee into giving us more treats!"

"Oh yeah?......What's your plan?"

"Follow my lead," she said.

Sweetie called an emergency meeting of the siblings and shared her plot with us.

"You see, Aimee doesn't know we understand about going potty outside. So, all we have to do is act like we're going to go potty inside! Then, when we get outside, just in the nick of time to go potty there, she'll give us a treat!"

Wow, it was great to have our big sister back with us. She really knew how to get the most out of every situation! Berry tried out Sweetie's plan first. He wandered by Aimee and started to hike his leg. Aimee screeched, "Oh no!," scooped Berry up and placed him outside. Berry went potty outside and wagged his tail all the while she praised him.

"Good boy, Berry!" Aimee exclaimed as she gave him a treat.

"What a great idea," Yippy squealed! "Yeah, that was great," Berry mumbled as he swallowed his cheese. "Got any other good ideas?"

One by one we pretended to forget where we were supposed to go potty, and one by one we got a treat when we went potty outside. Oh yes, this plan was working very, very well! It is best to work together! We were very happy, and we were getting very fat!

Chapter 4

Our New Purpose

"When are you going to give the pups away?" a neighbor asked, one afternoon.

"When I can find them good homes," Aimee replied. "I don't want to give them to just anyone. These pups are special, and they've had a rough start. I want to know their owners will treat them well."

"I know a family looking for a pup who would be a great owner," the neighbor said. "Can I bring them over to see the pups?"

"Sure. They can come over, but I don't want to give any of them away just yet. Tell them they can come by and get to know the pups. After I'm certain the pup they choose will be happy with them, they can have it," Aimee said.

The neighbor brought the family over. They seemed very nice and the little boy liked my brother, Berry. He cuddled with him, played with him, and petted him a lot. Berry liked him, too. He was happy to see him when he came back for another visit. After a couple of visits, Aimee let them take Berry home. She wanted to make sure the new owners really, really, really wanted Berry. Aimee figured if someone was willing to come back a couple of times to visit with us, they would be good owners. Aimee was sad to see Berry go, but she knew she couldn't take care of all of us forever.

"We promise to take very good care of Berry. Our son has already grown very fond of him. He'll be a good owner," the mother said.

"I believe that....but if you ever find you cannot keep him, please promise you'll bring him back to me," Aimee replied.

Berry was the first one of the siblings to have found a forever home. Aimee liked Berry's new family very much and knew he would have a happy life, but when he left, Aimee couldn't stop the tears from flowing.

I can't say I enjoyed going to the vet, but I admit he was quite kind. We all wanted to please Aimee and did our best to make a good impression, but I don't think we did a very good job. I confess I was very nervous and made a smelly mess....and Yippy was so scared she tried to bite him! And then, when we were leaving, I heard the vet tell Aimee she might want to give us some kind of medicine before she brought us there again so we would be calmer... Oh my..... there are going to be more of these trips????

"Sorry, young fellow," he said. "I have to give you a couple of vaccines so you'll stay healthy."

After a little while, he was done with me, and I was able to join my siblings out front.

"How was it?" Berry and Yippy asked.

"I didn't like the vacuum," I said.

"He vacuums you?" Yippy looked puzzled.

"No...well, it was something like that. It pinched!"

When we were all done, Aimee paid the bill with a credit card. I heard her tell the lady the doctor she worked for offered to pay the vet bills. Aimee told the lady sometimes it takes a village and that everybody was doing what they could to help us. The doctor had said he didn't have any time to care for us but offered to help by giving money.

"That's very generous of him," the lady said.

"Yes, yes, it is," Aimee replied.

Sweetie and Yippy

One day when Aimee was working in her office, a co-worker stopped in to visit.

"Hey Aimee, I've got the perfect adoptive parent for one of your pups," Karen said. "It's a friend of mine. She's got a heart of gold and has been looking for a new pup for a long time. I showed her a picture of the pups and she immediately fell in love with Sweetie. My friend says she's exactly what she's been looking for. Can I bring her by sometime?"

One evening, Karen and her friend came to our home. They stayed for hours. Her friend adored Sweetie and Sweetie liked her immediately, too. Aimee says there's someone for everyone. I think she's talking about people when she says that, but it seems to be true for pups too. Sweetie left that night with her new mom. I was sad to see my sister go, and I knew I was going to miss all the fun we had together, but I knew it was the best thing for her. I don't think dogs are meant to stay with each other. I think we're meant to love and care for people. Sweetie's new owner needed her, and I know Sweetie will be the best friend she's ever had.

After Sweetie left, it was just Yippy and me for a while until one night a young couple came over to meet us. They even brought a friend with them and they sat on the floor and talked for hours with Aimee. We cuddled, got petted a lot and played with them. We were still very shy around people, but while living at Aimee's house, we had learned there were lots of very kind and helpful people in the world.

The young couple had a hard time deciding which pup they wanted. I heard Aimee telling them that, from the very first time she found us, there was something special between Aimee and me. Oh, I was so happy to hear she felt that way! I didn't ever want to leave my new home!!

"You know, from the very first day I found them," Aimee said to the young couple, "I always felt that one chose me. In many ways, Happy is the most fearful, but he was the one who was willing to get the closest to me. There was something about me and something about my voice that drew him to me more than any of the other ones. I love all my porch puppies, but I don't think I can let him go."

"Oh, that works out perfectly!" exclaimed the young couple. "Happy is a sweet boy, but I think a girl pup is better for us."

When they left with Yippy that evening, they looked different. They had come to see us as a couple, but when they left with Yippy, they left as a family.

And We Lived Happily Ever After

My siblings and I had a rough start to life, but the kindness, helpfulness and generosity of strangers gave us wonderful lives with a purpose. Berry became a little boy's playmate, Sweetie became her mom's best friend, Yippy created a family for a young couple, and me, well Aimee tells me I'm her big boy.

The kindness of strangers taught me there are many important jobs to be done and that every act of kindness is important. People showed us kindness in different ways. Some people provided food, others provided money and others provided their time, but all the people who helped showed us their love by what they did. The world is a very different place to us now, and I think very differently about the people in it.

Love sure makes a big difference.

THE END

QUIZ:

1. Why did Aimee have to find homes for the porch puppies?

2. What should you let a dog do before petting one?

3. If you can't take care of a pet, what should you always do?

4. How did people help Aimee care for the puppies?

5. How did Happy get his name?

6. Why was Happy ignoring Sweetie when she first arrived at the house?

7. When the puppies learned to work together, what treat did they get?

8. How did the strangers show kindness to the puppies?

9. What did the kindness of strangers teach Happy?

10. Aimee says there's someone for everyone. How did each puppy complete their new family?

Then

Berry

Callie and Happy

Yippy

Sweetie

Today

Berry

Happy

Sweetie (Lucy)

Yippy (Winnie)

Author Bio

Elizabeth Stevens is a pianist who received her undergraduate degrees at Eastern New Mexico University and her graduate degree in piano performance from Southern Methodist University. She is a pianist in the Dallas area and has taught piano for over thirty years. Several years ago, she found four abandoned puppies. Her desire to write this book was a combination of her interest in educating children and a desire to share the wonderful message learned through this experience.

CPSIA information can be obtained
at www.ICGtesting.com
Printed in the USA
LVHW060346201020
669187LV00021B/159